Telling Stories

...in memory of us

D1445436

Cover Art:

"Absoultions...in the memory of Lee Morgan"
Acrylic on canvas
18" x 24"
Artist: Bus Howard

For Mom-
Who taught me that writing is more than putting
words on paper

For 'Cia-
My favorite dancer and my Spiritual Warrior

Thank you

To Kathy & Marty,

Thank you for all of your sharing & good vibrations!

Bright Moments

Telling Stories

…in memory of us

Bus Howard

Preface

I began writing these short stories in response to an article I read about one of my favorite writers, Alice Walker. She said that she wrote what she would like to read. I thought that that was a challenge. As a performer I use that same logic, I challenge myself to perform what I would like to see. Octavia Butler, helped me understand that science-fiction doesn't have to be relegated to just outer space and space travel. I had to ask myself what type of stories *I* would find interesting. Did *I* possess the chops necessary to deliver that kind of interest?

Two of my favorite musicians, Rahsaan Roland Kirk and Sun Ra, inspired me to create in words, what my ears experienced. I have never forgotten some of the acts that they put together to deliver their know-how. Aside from the incredible music they played, they created a climate of multi-sensory images that seemed to flow as one. In that regard, over the years, I have used some of these stories as *performance art pieces*. I blend live music, mostly the blues, and projected images to add a visual to the spoken word. My intent is to create (one day) as close as possible, an atmosphere of an "Old time Medicine Show"…complete with a barker shilling some potion that cures ills, grows hair, improves credit and renews good relations with in-laws. In this atmosphere, these stories are woven with a sound of music that is familiar to all. This is my attempt to bridge traditional African storytelling to American telling of tales.

As a Baby Boomer, I grew up with the television shows of, The Twilight Zone, The Outer Limits and One Step Beyond. The stories told made me wonder… What If? My interest in quantum physics and meta-physics inspired many of the stories I have written. Out of ordinary situations something extraordinary happens and how will the characters react. In those moments of déjà vu, moments when time appears to stand still or warp, what exactly has occurred? I pray that the reader finds some story here that stretches their imagination in the same way. Who knows, maybe one day that person on the other side of the mirror will wink at you. Bright moments!

In Africa every morning a gazelle awakens knowing that it must outrun the fastest lion if it wants to stay alive.
Every morning a lion wakes up knowing that it must run faster than the slowest gazelle or it will starve to death.
It makes no difference whether you are a lion or a gazelle; when the sun comes up, you had better start running.

-African Proverb

Ascension

Laughing Horse wasn't laughing now; the noon sun bore down on him relentlessly. The matter at hand was for him to get through this part of the supplication, and he couldn't remember if he had been unconscious. The Full Moon Medicine Wheel that he was a part of encompassed his entire being. He hadn't been in his body for what seemed an eternity. Had it been seven days or seventeen? He couldn't remember. Where was the cougar that had been with him last night? Jumping Elk was the initial spiritual guide but he hadn't remembered seeing him either. They spoke the same language, the same words, as they sat in the sweat lodge, but this isn't the sweat lodge. Was the sweat lodge a figment of his imagination also? This part of the ritual was foretold as the most trying, trying it was.

His body was now almost completely off the ground, tethered by the drying sinews on his wrists and ankles. As the sun reached its zenith the tethers pulled tighter. It's difficult to imagine how, he alone, set himself in this position. This position is the one that the mother earth can not ignore; it is of divine remorse and petition. His prayers will be heard, this he is assured, but will his sins be forgiven. A few carved barite roses are scattered around for the warriors who are no longer confined to the physical plane. It is said that the warriors return at night to carve the roses. The desert roses are scattered so the location of the warrior's meeting places will continue to be known only to those who are able to leave...this space. The message from the energy that the desert rose has is the most scared areas of ones life are those in which ancient hatred has been transformed into present love. This is what Laughing Horse is betting on, betting his life on...that sacred area of ancient hatred... this present love.

Laughing Horse had been despondent as he headed for the stream that meandered through the village. This had been a bountiful year harvest and people-wise, the Elders felt added security was needed to the rear flanks. This type of work was usually given to lesser young men in the village, Laughing Horse felt slighted; besides this was to be the first hunt of the season and he wouldn't be in it. They were to find fresh ponies, the symbol of good fortune and luck in the eyes of The

Great Spirit...and he wasn't going. He was to add his skills as a tried and tested warrior...watching women and children work and play, with this thought he spat upon the ground. He knew in his heart he must be humble, but this didn't diminish the extreme feelings he was having.

As dusk fell he could hear the whoops and shouts from the arriving warriors. He was certain Sitting Water would rub in his face the events, assuredly embellished, for his benefit. He wanted no part of this, as his replacement approached; Laughing Horse mounted his pony and headed for the sunset. The stream that ran through the village turned back on itself about 5 miles from his home. It ran off to a small waterfall, in a clump of thick woods the base of which provided a spectacular view of the sunset. He tied his mount, removed his buckskins and entered the water. At the exact same moment a maiden was removing her garments and entering the same water just down stream, making the exact same sounds. It had been a moment or two before they felt each, then saw each other, naked and alive. If they were startled it didn't show, it was more of the feeling of recognizing someone you've never seen, yet knew personally. As her gaze fixed on him for what seemed an endless time, Laughing Horse grew hard and erect. As his gaze fixed on her, Running Doe felt her body slowly heating, juices flowing, slowly with deliberation; they drew near each other, and without a word became lovers.

Spent and in each others arms between the shore and the shallow water, the mist of the waterfall's cooling vapors on their bodies, a bird's call from the bushes made Running Doe scamper to her garments. Without so much as a look behind her, fate was sealed between these two. Who was she? What was her name? Where is she from? Laughing Horse returned to his belongings and headed for his village. As he approached he sensed the danger in the air, his warrior training prepared him for moments like these. The Elders had already gathered the warriors of his age were assembled ready to ride. The replacement to Laughing Horse's post had been killed, killed in an attempted raid on the village's new arrival of ponies. He had been asleep and the invaders crept up on him, startled him and he slipped and fell from his perch. He broke his neck in the fall. As senseless as it was, Laughing Horse felt responsible, if only he'd said something to the young man before leaving the post. Something like what, he thought? He didn't know.

As he entered the circle of warriors, Sitting Water with his back to him, turned and said aloud "Your soul will never rest for the death of that young one." A challenge directed towards him, a direct challenge. How should he respond to this, how would he save face implicated with this young one's death? Though it was not his responsibility for the duty watch of the young one, a warrior of his status and rank should never have had something like this occur. Laughing Horse's heart hardened at the words. Without hesitating he unsheathed his knife, threw it into the earth, answering the challenge with one of his own. The other warriors in unison scrambled between these foes before something got out of hand. Reminding both of the current events cooled their heads off momentarily. In that moment, though, the eyes of those two told tales of past slights, both real and imagined between them. If looks could kill-two looks-two dead. Jumping Elk came running toward the group with something in his hand. In the dark, he'd found a beaded bag dropped from one of the raiders. Jumping Elk got his name for his superior eyesight and cunning, he could track anything on any surface, for any amount of time. This bag was all that he would need for tracking down and punishing the invaders. Without haste the warriors mounted and the searched started. Sitting Water and Jumping Elk rode toward the river; Laughing Horse bringing up the rear wanted nothing to do with his foe. Sometime before dawn Laughing Horse saw in the distant horizon two riders and two people on foot behind them approaching. It was Sitting Water and Jumping Elk with prisoners tied by their wrist tethered behind them. As they came into focus he could tell that one of the prisoners was a woman, it was...noooo! It was Running Doe, now a captive. His silent shout of no, froze Sitting Water on his mount. Froze him to the point that his heart stopped still, he dropped like a heavy load from his pony dead to the ground. Jumping Elk didn't know what to make of this occurrence, as the sun rose on these four with the dead warrior; a party was riding hard toward them. Laughing Horse made no attempt to flee; his heart and his soul were exposed at this moment. As the riders advanced, Laughing Horse cut the tethers from the prisoners and told Jumping Elk that there must have been some kind of mistake, for he knew this woman. Before the response could come from Jumping Elk, they all became caught in the excitement of Running Doe's search party. With one gesture Running Doe stopped her warriors in their tracks, saying that these two had saved her life from the potential kidnapper. In seconds, Laughing Horse and Jumping Elk were on top of shoulders, cheered to the heavens. They were invited to be received by her village Elders for a celebration. The daughter of the Chief and niece of the Medicine Man had been found unharmed, great cause for celebration. The looks that these lovers shared toward each other, removed any doubt that they were connected. The hardness in the heart of Laughing Horse as he gazed upon the deceased Sitting Water showed all of the bitterness and confusion he harbored. A good warrior had fallen and again he felt responsible, was it him and his thoughts that killed Sitting Water? From outward appearances he had had nothing to do with his demise. In his heart he knew he was responsible, even if Jumping Elk didn't.

After much food and laudatory words about these two, Laughing Horse was asked if he had any special request from his hosts, nothing was too much to ask for. The request that he made surprised all that were near. He wanted her uncle, the Medicine Man, to help him purge from his soul the guilt, the bad medicine, he was feeling. This seemingly unselfish act endeared him immediately to all. This man had asked for cleansing of his soul, instead of riches or wives, surely he was a wise man. A sweat lodge was set up in his honor, and the sacred Full Moon Medicine Wheel was prepared. His request to appeal to the Great Spirit by himself in the Full Moon Medicine Wheel, brought oohs and aahs from the gathered. No one could remember anyone in their days that experienced this type of ceremony alone. It could kill a man in a short while from exposure. Why would he they thought? Who was he? Where was he from?

Tied spread eagle on the ground, the energy from the barite roses around him stimulates vision, enhances friendship, harmony, love and provides insight into the relationship connection. These qualities he was counting on. He had been raised by the teachings of the Great Spirit...seek first the kingdom of heaven...and all things will be made unto you. Focused with this thought, his spirit returned to the waterfall, there the spirits of Running Doe and Laughing Horse embraced.

Shape-shifter

Fella named Einstein put it like dis...cain't no two people be at the same place at the same time...that's what she wanted me to be. See, she could shape-shift when she wanted to and thought, naw, expected, those close to her do the same. She'd say, "How long a'time you been seeing me do this, and you still ain't figured out how, yet?" Like I'm stupid or something. It ain't like I'm not tryin'...'cause I am. It's really something to see, *I* just ain't figured out how to do it yet. That's the part she had the problem with. When we met, we knew immediately who each other was. We had been waiting for these spirits to link-up. The relationship that took course was one as spiritual partners. Effortless and at the same time quite a bit of work. Operating from a higher plane, relationship-wise...well...that brings on another dimension. Our norm was *thought* first, then verbal response. We both knew it's not by chance this happens, it's the course from there, I'm talking about. Like the days that you don't want to be 'read'. The days you'd kill for some bar-b-qued ribs and some cold kool-aid. See, you know that's wrong, but you go there, anyway.

I don't remember when I noticed that she was getting good at doing it. It's just that she'd be gone longer and longer periods of time. Not gone, as in away spiritually, I only have to "buzz her up "on the vibe line to feel her, to get her. She used to laugh and say, "I'm not-deaf... you don't have to holler". Just a mere thought, better still, a gentle thought, is all that is necessary to reach her. Now, I wouldn't know what to say...that hasn't already been said. Yeah...I guess I do miss her smell and seeing her physically, though from time to time we visit through fragrances. We made a promise when we first met, to always strive to recognize each other, no matter what life-form we may assume. No matter what system we may be on and that we are eternally linked. I never knew how those words would become so true.

I was the one that started having the 'flying dreams' first. We went to a holistic health fair in the country and met this Native American. When he saw her, he said something in her ear. She responded in his native language...how she knew it...surprised even her. She touched his forehead. He'd recently been on a vision quest and spoke with her then; I mean she'd been his guide through it, though this was the first time they were meeting physically. I'd never known her to lay hands on any stranger, but she reached over his display table and concocted a bunch of herbs, lit them, breathed in the aromas, then blew them in his face gently. The smoke turned a light blue, and she again chanted in native tongue for a few moments. Then they were gone. It wasn't like magic; I felt them leave before they did. I knew they were gone, but hadn't left me. It was a suspension in time, is the best way for me to explain it. That's the way it was explained to me. She returned a few hours later, at home. I had just finished eating dinner and she appeared between the kitchen and dining room, with the most incredible tan...glow is a better word. I asked what had happened and she began to explain it in that language that I couldn't understand, let alone begin to mimic. I'd never heard that sound come out of a human body before. It was the only way she could tell me she said. This was the way to explain it she told me. As my dreams of flying increased, her voyages, as she put it, became more and more frequent. It's here in front of you she'd say, trust yourself, use what you have to access your potential...and lighten up. I think my expression of disbelief would betray me, as the senses I've trusted for so long had. I had no way to explain this...to anyone...other than her. What would I say? "Hey Mom, you'd never guess who can fly" Well, the time spent in this plane started to become less and less. The way that was explained to me, the correct terms would be more and more. It's the way in which energy is used to its potential. More and more seemed less and less to me, in the old way of thinking. In the old way of seeing, with my eyes that is. Before I saw her last, she told me think of a radio, we as radios. We are sending and receiving machines, and at certain frequencies we are received and we are sent. This is how it's done. The lessons to be learned are many and time is how we use it...think right and we can fly...the kingdom of heaven is within. And she was.

The Grace of Fate

He casually scanned the groceries in front of his, and made the last thought audible, "I sure don't miss those days"as he looked over her groceries. "Excuse me", the voice said, snapping him out of his mental dreamscape. He looked up to see...those eyes...those eyes of his dreams for the last month or so. Could it be, right here in front of me, he thought? With this thought, he became aware that his stare was making her uncomfortable. "Oh, I was just thinking out loud, it's a bad habit of mine", he said. "I'm all up in your groceries", but this time he did see in her eyes, and she saw him seeing in her eyes, but didn't bother to deny that something was definitely there between them. She reached over her things to get the plastic divider to separate his stuff from hers and her hand brushed his. At that same moment, in Jamaica, a clap of thunder and a flash of lightening erupted through the sky. He impulsively grabbed her hand, gently pulled her closer to him and kissed her lightly on the lips. A squall blew through the sky over the tropical island that both of them imagined. At this magical instant. A romantic interlude in the checkout lane of the local mega-chain food store. Before either of them could react they drew back from each other, looking shocked, and then threw themselves at each other with a knowing, that those behind them in line could only postulate, they did indeed know each other, and this interlude was a game being played, for all on-lookers benefit. In fact, the lady that was three people down in line, didn't think much of this happenstance at all, "get on with it", she said under her breath, "Take that mushiness outside". This was exactly what they were doing, though at this time neither of them knew it, yet. Their spirits, knew before they did, had met halfway between these two and carried on something fierce, I'm talking off the scale... before these two met physically, but in that dimension scales don't exist, it's just a way to explain it as close as I can. It's no wonder these two reacted the way that they did. She'd walked to the store and was thinking before he said that out loud about her groceries that she could go for a ride back home right about now. He was thinking, before the grocery blurt-out, of how he'd like to have someone riding with him, in his new car, in his new city. See, I'm talking match from the beginning, spirit-linked these two were.

As he made his way around the car, letting himself in, after opening her side door, he slid his lanky body under the wheel as her hand slid between the unbuttoned buttons of his shirt and pinched his nipple...hard. All he could moan was...aww girl. It was on. It's the memory of those first hot wet kisses that take it to the next level, always. You know how someone's tongue in your mouth couldn't be juicer, their saliva like nectar, mixing with yours, creating lubricating fluids for the words to slid out your mouths into each others ears, causing friction, causing motion, cause and effect.

They would laugh and joke about who would be the first one to just up and disappear, after coming. They often recalled in their memories of those first few encounters, the dimensional traveling and learning, on such different levels. This was the direct after-result of their shared body experiences. It felt that good; shoot still does, as they tell it. Early one morning, the first morning he spent at her place, he awoke and began to tell her in the most delicious way how he felt about her, in Spanish. It brought tears to her eyes. She looked at his mouth and his teeth as he was saying these beautiful things to her. She didn't know what he was saying...

but there was no doubt she knew what he meant...every word...every Spanish word...that was coming out of his mouth so smoothly, like silk feels, like satin looks... hypnotic and oh so exotic. Make you moist...it did. That's why it took her so long to comment on his ability to speak Spanish so smoothly. When they regained themselves, from her showing him her appreciation of those words, is that your native language," she asked? What chu talkin' 'bout...English? He said and looked perplexed, he wasn't getting it. She realized something incredible had happened...again. She said, "The Spanish you just spoke so fluently". He opened his mouth to speak, telling her how much...and again in fluent Spanish, out came the words. He really wasn't aware that he was speaking in another language, he later told her he was only expressing what was on his heart. He told her of how, after he was in that "just came real good" sleep, he dreamt he'd been a warrior... in some other time...with her...them making love...and as they re-connected at her house in this time, he got his memory back. He said he couldn't feel any difference in his thinking, that he's speaking Spanish, it seems as though he's thinking in English. "I always wanted to speak another language; I just didn't think I'd learn it over night." Effortlessly he explained, in a diatribe of flowing Spanish that only made her blush. She had to kiss him after that. It was only a matter of time before *she* began to manifest the energy of their combination.

Her manifestation came in the least expected place... the work place. In the middle of her 6th period class, it hit her. Hit her smack in the middle of her morality. "What am I doing?" she said. "Throw those books in the trash, right over there, right now", she said to her Honors class. "I'm sorry" she told them, "Either I have to quit this position or I have to teach from another viewpoint, starting right now." We're going to take this class from a knowledge based curriculum to a values-based curriculum. "Who knows anything about *power?*" she stated. "What's the difference in creating your own reality or accepting the reality you've created?" that's homework for tonight. Those two questions got her almost-tenured-self, suspended from classroom teaching for two months. These two questions shook up the administration of the prestigious academy where she taught. "It wasn't in the course directive" is what she was told. She saw things differently right then and there, clearly, what she had to do, her life mission. The pretense of being culture free, politically correct, unbiased, and therefore able to objectively analyze others cultures, is an illusion that distorts any real understanding of diversity. She was having no more of that in her life. Her light was on...beaming.

A grocery store meeting, a good hook-up, destined to happen. Their delicious moments caused shifts in the San Andreas Fault. Where do you think El Nino came from? As my Uncle used to say, "Might could be." But combined energies is what we're talking about here. They literally moved mountains. She got her cousins to speak to each other again. Just from the glow he and she had. When these two walked in, under the tent, where the food was spread, all eyes were on them. While she was introducing him, at the family reunion, these cousins who hadn't spoken since her grandparents' time, mouths dropped open. "Who are these two glowing, like this?" The two cousins said, to each other, without thinking that they weren't speaking, at the same time. It made them both laugh at the happenstance. The love warmed their hardened hearts.

I tell you this kind of thing happened everywhere these two went. As they both grew more aware of the reality that they created, their power was astonishing.

They moved mountains. Last I talked to them, they told me this story again, about how they met, in person. The different occurrence was that in the retelling, they hadn't opened their mouths to tell me. Yet I heard every word, it was the coolest thing. I had to write it down.

Ithiopia

As we approached the border, Abibi had to reassure me again, that if I tell him one more time he's not going in the right direction...besides his cousins were the border guards...again he told me, relax, I'd need all my attentions to stay focused for what was at hand. I'd also lost my passport during our trek through the desert, no passport, no visa, no real ID to speak of. I said, if I could get to an embassy, I'd get all of this settled. This was of no importance now, I'd been told. My life was to change forever, in fact it already had.

A little more than a month ago, a few Niabinghi Rasta brothers and I thought that a pilgrimage to Ithiopia would do us some spiritual good. We contacted some countrymen to help us make this journey special. We decided that a trek through the desert would give us a feeling of the true pilgrimage to the Holy of Holies. We didn't know how we'd be received by the Elders, but we knew that our hearts were fixed and our minds were regulated to the truth we sought. As night fell in the desert on our seventh evening, I took my customary walk after dinner to reflect, I was led to a space about a mile from camp. I could see the glow from the campfire over my shoulder, the shadow that it cast in front of me led me to the small opening in the cave that I would have otherwise missed. This small opening in the dune held a small barreled chest. This was the stuff *Arabian Nights* was made of, I thought. When I caught my breath and beheld the chest, I experienced an electrical feeling that pulsed through my body. The next thing I remembered everyone was standing over me saying they'd seen the most incredible light come from this direction. Was I all right? I assured them I was, wasn't I? Where was the chest? It had buried itself under my body as I was now lying prone on the desert floor. As they raised the lantern to inspect my face, they all stood back with awe as they focused on my forehead. From where I was laying or fell on the chest, an insignia that was an ancient Coptic Cross was now on my forehead. It wasn't tattooed, or pressed; it was more like a very detailed birthmark, clearly a part of my skin. I couldn't remember if this insignia was on the chest when I first picked it up, though it wasn't on there now. I said, no one was to open the chest, for this is how I was instructed. Abibi left to spread the news ahead of this occurrence; surely we would be received by the Elders now.

Abibi arrived back at the camp site just before dawn; he'd been instructed to bring me to the sacred Temple of the Living Stone. He said the messengers had to take this story to the Council, which no one man alone could directly approach.

Abibi was advised to instruct me how to respond in the native tongue to chants and prayers until I was conversant enough to lead them; I had no idea what I was saying at first. Next, came the daily anointing with oils and swaddling in fine linens (that I didn't even know we were carrying). This became the first order of business each day and the close of each evening. These rituals, as they became, were of utmost importance I was told. We were racing to be prepared to be received by the Elders.

It's now been two weeks since I first beheld the chest; it seems everyone in camp this morning is a bit salty with me. I'm also being treated differently by the countrymen, that are accompanying us on this journey. Most of this has to do with my inadvertently taking them all with me on a vision quest I had last night. I am now the topic of discussion behind hands to mouths. I know this. I don't think most of them appreciated the way that they were whisked into the past, into the times of the Abyssinians. It seems that if I dream or think about something intensely enough, I can astral travel to any place or time. And as I found out last night, I can transport others with me. We arrived right in the line of fire and arrows, at a battle that was pitched at this location centuries ago. The countrymen were taking quite a beating and my Rasta brothers were my aids and under-generals. I had the position as commander, with chariots and fine horses at my disposal, I commanded three companies on the outer fringes in addition to my charges, all the while giving orders simultaneously. At the very moment we were surrounded, by the yet unseen enemy, I realized the reason I was leading this battle. I gave orders to charge, then, we all awoke this morning...from the same dream...exhausted and soaked from night sweats. When it was realized that all had had the same dream experience, all eyes fixed on me. When I opened my mouth to speak a clap of thunder and a bolt of lightning erupted at the same time drowning out my words. I raised my arms to...and a pulse of energy escaped from my fingers to fork through the sky in a yellow web of static electricity. This display brought all to their knees in front of me, and humbled me in the same manner. I couldn't explain this. Just like I couldn't explain how my hands got tattooed, like the women's hands we saw in that village. I woke up and this is how they were, tattooed indigo-blue. I was told that this practice of dye came from the ancient Hindus, what it means for me I haven't yet figured out.

Each day this land reveals something else to me through its oracles. I'm learning how to read the signs, that will enable us to *make it through*. This "*make it through*" part isn't yet connected in my conscience. When I mediate about it all I see is nothing, like looking at a blank wall. Yet I feel it has something to do with *making it through*.

The stories of this land come to me in my dreams and in my meditations. The sons of Noah, Ham and Shem are the fathers of this land, the Hamites and Semites have lived on this earth, this land, with its plagues and famines. The story of how the finest ruler this world has ever known, Sheba, was tricked by Solomon, into giving it up, which begot Menelik I. These people's strength's, resistances, beauty and devout spirit continue to show through. I'm connected to this, all of this. I can hardly recognize the person in me that started this trek weeks ago. Is this the spirit that is leading me I wonder? I see this space where we are to wait, after we have cleansed our thoughts, and supplicated ourselves to be received. This is why I keep telling Abibi this doesn't look familiar to me...the centuries have changed the land patterns.

I'm making everyone quite testy nowadays between the visions and electrical lightshows I seem to produce at will. I think it's like being with someone you don't know, if you should fear or adore, that fine line. I tell them it's temporary, I'm only being used, led, directed, however they can synthesize it...that's what's going on. I sleep alone now in a tent. Those who used to sleep around me say I have no problem in taking occupants near me on these dreamscapes, and they're not as sure as I seem to be on these voyages, that they're in control. I tell them that I'm not in control, but this doesn't seem to calm anyone enough to want to sleep near me. They also say in the wee hours, intense light and faint music comes from my tent, with the aromas of fine perfumes, it's almost as if the entire tent has a huge fan inside, billowing it out. I ask why no one has entered when this experience happens, I'm told when one walks up on it, the next thing is that they are standing in the desert by themselves, as if the tent didn't exist. Yet when they return to a certain distance away from it, it reappears. I tell them, "Be not afraid, we're in good hands that are leading us to where we are to be...making it through. It still doesn't feel like it's supposed to...yet, as dusk falls on this beautiful savanna, calmness prevails. We are near the border.

With much trepidation the border crossing went on without incident, the clear morning sky directed our feet to the edge of the first cliff we were to cross. I told Abibi I know a shortcut that will save us time and distance. The chasm seemed impassable to the naked eye, the early morning ground fog gave the vista an other-worldly persona. Abibi asked if I were sure we were here so soon. I assured him that we were. I suggested that we make camp and prepare ourselves for the final journey. We settled down on the precipice of the outer banks of this mountain face. I began to feel excited that we had reached our destination. With a small electrical charge I emitted from my person we were glided across the expanse. The spiritual side of our excursion was to begin after morning vespers and a bath of pure water. With no water in sight I knew we were to experience another miracle, for indeed they do happen everyday. The call to prayer took on a new meaning to me and directed and focused our combined energy. *Making it through* was what this was about.

What started as a low murmur, increased to a dull tremble, it seemed as though the earth under us was beginning to move. At that moment, on the narrow ledge that we were on, an opening appeared in the face of the mountain. We had been standing at the opening of the path, yet it had not revealed itself to us until our invocations were completed. A doorway, just wide enough for us to pass through sideways appeared. In the image of the Coptic Cross that was on my forehead. Inside was a cavern of magnificent size and proportions, with a natural waterfall tinted by filtered light from a source unknown. This light cast the most serene and peaceful radiance I have ever experienced. We were now inside of the mountain, the living stone, we lowered ourselves into the water and the opening that had been was no more. Instinctively the group went through the falls to a path that was centuries old, hewn from the travel of feet of pilgrims like ourselves. These paths connected us to more paths, some we knew were dead ends and others that connected to sacred places. As we trod along, locations of past events that happened in this space made themselves known to us. The beneficent Queen of Sheba brought her entourage here to refresh them for their journey to meet Solomon. This is where the Levites camped when they brought the Ark of the Covenant. During the Italian occupation this is where H.I.M. (His Imperial Majesty-Haile Selassie), hid and fought from. As we reached the inner sanctum, we looked upon each other and realized collectively, there were no doors or openings in this room, we had traveled through stone, rock. Made it through. From the shoulders of giants, we are now perched taller. Sette Massagana.

The Uncontrolled Waste

As he looked out of the window on the magnificent view, he couldn't help but wonder if this might be the last look he would have on his beautiful native land. Tears welled up in his eyes as he went on a trip through his memory, of his past and present, on this land. The male dominated side of his consciousness quickly took over returning him dry eyed to the present. The matter at hand was to coordinate his highly clandestine departure from the political and social strife that was plaguing his country. This strife, having to do directly, with the economic collapse, recently experienced by the hard working and thrifty people. This collapse, brought about wholly by the repeated theft of funds sponsored by his regime. The rich did indeed get richer and the poor got systematically poorer. As social services decreased, the military-style police became more and more severe. The local press had been censored to the point of interrogations and brutal punishments, those dissidents who braved the authorities and spoke out about the abuses, rarely were seen or heard from again. My grandmother called it a "pot 'bout to boil over". It surely was.

The crucial matter was the transportation of currency and gold bullion that was going with him personally. Who he could trust would be of concern for so far he hadn't let on to anyone his plan. Would he dispose of the carriers and porters once the shipment reached its final destination? So much to think about and how had it gotten to this point he thought? It had been said in that "trouble-maker's" play that the demise began when he'd jailed his father for speaking out publicly against his regime. What else was I to do he thought? He broke the law in my face, my law. He himself always taught me that when you break the law knowingly, knowingly a man will stand to answer his infraction. This is all that I had done, he thought, who would have known he would slip and fall down the stairs. Yes, it looked suspicious, but I was there.

From the moment of his conception he was called Allumede, most awaited one. The raising of the royal one went without a hitch. The proper schooling and decorum agreed with his personality. He was a trained leader, natural and hardworking. The fact that he remained a single man added a degree of daring to his good looks and family name. My grandmother said, power corrupts, and absolute power corrupts absolutely. The climb up the political and social ladder could not have been staged on a grander level. All the 'i's were dotted and all the 't's were crossed. At the coronation, as President-for-life, in the distance, muffled shots rang out into the bodies of the last rebels who would raise arms against his government. A sort of ringing out the old, and bringing in the new. An uneven trade as the history of this land unfolds.

The celestial alignment at the conception of his birth coincided with an event that occurred on this earth in the same location centuries before. The karmic play out began to unfold as he made the final plans for his escape. The energies of thoughts began to formulate, create and promulgate. The eddies and whirlpools of this energy began it's spiral and concentrated into a vortex opening that reached out to other linking energies and snowballed itself into the mass of pure psychic plasma. When it hit him he went into another state momentarily. Thinking that he had had a dizzy spell from the extreme pressure he'd been under, he sat on the steps in the hallway of the secret passage that led to the airfield, gathering himself.

Sitting on the airstrip was his Gulfstar V private jet, fueled and loaded with what he'd need for exile. As he approached, from the bushes 50 meters ahead, sprang a leopard that charged straight at him, stopped in its tracks a few meters from him and dropped dead. A discharge came from the leopard that immediately a tracker that had chased it from the bush was rubbing on his hands. Who was he and where did he come from that his guards hadn't intercepted him? The tracker looked into his eyes at that moment, stood and rubbed this mixture on his palms and blew the gooey substance into the direction of the escaping monarch. The stench clung to his uniform and skin like a bad habit, with it the thought came into his mind, "Hueval and Hueval Ltd., Geneva, Switzerland. As he blinked his eyes to avoid the spray in his face, he refocused and the tracker was gone, along with the carcass of the leopard.

The odor of the gooey spray permeated the interior of the jet. It reeked of decomposing flesh, concentrated and odorous, nauseating. He removed his garments and discarded them on the tarmac before take-off. This act didn't remove the stench that remained on his skin, by osmosis-adhered. After showering he was able to put enough cologne on himself to withstand this new odor. Who was that person, that tracker? The bounty of gold bullion that he offered for the capture of that tracker will number his days, assuredly, he mused. He will pay with his life for desecrating my person, he spat.

The landing was as smooth as he had ever experienced, it seemed as though he was being led. A limousine waited as he deplaned, he couldn't remember making these details. The driver called for him by the new name he was assuming. How could this be? No time to dally here in sight, he thought. The driver's only words were, he knew the way to Hueval and Hueval, the financial offices of the Limited, Hueval and Hueval, Swiss Bankers, Geneva Switzerland, were requirements met? Anything else? Who was he? This was all happening so fast that it felt all right, no internal alarms went off...go with the flow he felt. As the limo neared the destination he felt lighter, he smelled his skin and wondered if he was beginning to smell better, was this imagination? He felt rested for the first time in recent memory as they neared the building, the reality of his saga hit home with him as he stepped out of the limo. The air smelled clearer and his hopes rose anew for a brighter future. The transactions took place without delays or encumber-ments. Now his stolen fortunes secured in this Swiss bank, he felt assured. As he exited the bank to find lodging for the evening his thoughts drifted to his homeland and country, the odor from his encounter with the tracker returned with force unknown to him. Each thought of reprisal to his enemies increased the foul smell on his person until people on the street turned their noses up from him. As he entered the hotel, his bowels let loose and the escaping smell was more pungent that he had ever encountered. The management did their level best to whisk him into the first available room away from the other guests. Within days he was asked to leave the premises because of the stench. With each thought of his ensconced funds, his bodily functions would lose their hold and he would embarrass himself wherever he was. This also held true with any thoughts he would have of his country, position or past royalty. He became a prisoner of his thoughts; nowhere could he be allowed to stay for any period of time before the odor would turn others away from him. If he thought of obtaining his funds from the bank, he would immediately urinate on himself with such force that he would dehydrate. If he found himself going in the general direction of the bank, his bowels would let loose the foulest substance, until it became clear that he must be cursed. He became a person of the streets. The further his thoughts took him from his past wrongs and mismanagement the better he felt and smelled, but a moment of thought would return with fury and vengeance the odor now associated with his past wrongs. The simplest function took a concentrated effort beginning with pure thought and ending with the same. A prisoner, in his own body, jailed by his mind, sentenced by past misdeeds.

Reuters News Service- The Swiss Financial offices of Hueval and Hueval announced that funds in an account, in excess of 2.3 billion marks have sat in their deposit for over 25 years, untouched. No activity of any kind has ever happened since it's deposit. If anyone has any information, please contact...

...as his eyes scanned the notice, in the paper that covered his face from the morning sun, a warm trickle of urine flowed down his leg.

Slapped into Next Week

You know how it's not until a few seconds later that the body actually registers that something unusual has just happened, like that girl just slapped that other girl. You know you heard the sound and out of the corner of your eye you thought you saw…and sure enough, that was what happened. Slapped her so hard, it was like my mother used to say, "Slapped her into the middle of next week". That's exactly where she woke up, somewhere around Wednesday or Thursday. She wasn't out that long or in a coma; she was slapped into a time warp. She thought she was falling, like in a dream, but events were whirring by her at such speed all she could do was hold on…mentally.

My brother, Junior, was now standing in front of her at her front door, saying, "Oh…I gotta come over here too and get you, for you to give me a little help. What you forgot it's Wednesday?" Now I know I'm tripping, Wednesday? What happened to the weekend? Wait, all I remember, I was at the grocery store and this bitch was all up in my face talkin' 'bout…

"You gonna go with me or what," Junior almost screamed at me, snapping me out of that dreamscape… "huh? Wha? oh yeah…let me get my things, where are my car keys?" "Your car keys, Junior laughed, what are you talking about? You better than anyone knows what happened to that. Shit girl, now you really trippin', that wasn't 48 hours ago and now you got convenient amnesia? You something else, c'mon now, let's go before you got me running late. They say you gotta strike while the iron is hot. Now remember what we went over, just give them the plain facts, I've got the money in a cashier's check for the balance, all you do is what we rehearsed…got it?" Hell I don't have a clue as to what Junior is talking about, what happened to the last few days? When did I put this outfit on, a business suit? What time is it? "Nicole…Nikki…let's go now!" Junior shouted.

For a young man, Junior drove like he was seventy, complete stops at stop signs, always put his blinkers on and he drove reeeaalll sloooow. What did I get myself into? Junior is the financial wiz in our family; he set up a family investment plan a few years ago and so far my portion of the dividends has paid my mortgage for the year. He won't say how much money he has amassed in his young life but he's set, so what I've agreed to is anyone's guess.

I'm trying hard to remember the last thoughts I had before now, am I dreaming? I pinched myself way too hard and blurted out loud…"ouccchhh!" Junior glanced over at me with a look that didn't deny his displeasure. How do I get him to talk about the events of these past few days without coming off as the only flake? "Junior, what do you think happened to my car, since you're so concerned?" "Me, concerned, I could care less about you and your shenanigans". With that he hit the "Onstar" button on his dashboard and proceeded to make his hands free call. I knew better than to speak at this moment with him taking care of business. If I could get a newspaper I could see some of the events that have taken place and that might jar my memory. What happened? I have absolutely no recollection of the past few days. Wait…if I could get the daily numbers I could make a mint with previous knowledge, but that's assuming that I could go back to that time again. Oh, I am tripping; tears welled up in my eyes without a moment's notice. Junior looked at me and said, "Hey guys, I'll call you back in ten, something's come up with my sister that needs my immediate attention." Just like Junior, he put on his emergency blinkers and pulled over to the shoulder of the road. "Do you need to talk to a therapist, I was sure you would have mentioned the break-up by now." Break-up? I almost screeched, I had to swallow hard, okay, breathe now…1,2,3… breathe…I broke up? I hadn't even thought about my boyfriend until now, and we've broken up? A smile crept across my lips subconsciously, wow! What all could happen in, what is it, five days it's been?

"Okay, Junior I said, you won't believe this but the last few days have been such a blur that I don't remember nothing. He sat there and looked at me for at least a minute without saying a thing, looking right through me. "What's not to believe, he finally said. I'd of had the same reaction myself, I'm sure…so you're okay?" He looked at me again and before I could answer he signaled to return to traffic as if he'd answered all of the questions in my mind.

This is so difficult; I don't remember ever having no recall of past events. That has always been my strong suit, being able to remember the minutest detail. If I can remember the day, I can associate the weather, people and events tied to it. With this I can't remember a thing.

This girl was all up in my face talking about how she was gonna...riiinnngggggggg...the alarm clock shocked me out of that reality and what was that crazy dream I just had...wait Junior was in it and I couldn't remember...I can't remember what just took place, what was that? I

can't remember...I can't remember...I...I...I.

...This is how it ends

As he walked away from the drawer, where you put your money, at the gas station, I saw his face. I saw him close up; I could point him out in a line-up if it came to that. But, I saw him none the less, and he saw me seeing him. If I were not my mother's son, I wouldn't be in this situation. My mother *was* the nosey lady on the block. You could see her if you looked up in our window. She was the one peeking from the sides of the curtains...like you couldn't see her. The thing that always gave her away was her commentary- out of the window. "Honey, she waited out front for...'bout an hour...for you", "Say, you boys...don't hit those cars with those sticks" "I just know on your way back... you're gonna pick up that trash you dropped...right?"

I shouldn't have looked at him so closely. I watched him like I was 5-O. He picked that up. I 'm not ready...they say you always know when it's your time.

That's why my heart skipped a beat as I drove up. I was supposed to sign papers this week, for insurance, a goodly amount for the family, if something were to happen to me. Now look at me...directly in harms way. Oh...I miss the kids so much already...and my soul mate...why?

If you're gonna do me, c'mon and get it over with. I remember once, my sister had some guy follow her into our apartment building on Oglesby. Little did he know that eight real big guys were having a meeting upstairs. She came upstairs all excited, talking 'bout how this guy was following her and she had her back all tightened up for the knife he was sure to plant in there any moment. It never happened...the knife part. But he *was* in the kitchen, downstairs, with Momma, our grandmother. She thought my sister knew this guy, and she was going upstairs to get me to see her friend. My cousin Dwayne asked the guy who he was and what was he doing in his cousin's kitchen. The guy goes mongoloid on us...no understand English. Dwayne throws the guy pretty much through the door. Picks him up by his hair and tosses him down a flight of stairs, following him closely, to whup his ass at the bottom of the steps. This guy does a thing like in the cartoons...

jumps up in the air, then starts his legs running before he hits the ground...I swear, I saw it...I was right there. Its funny how I'm thinking of all this stuff, in so short a time span, he's almost right up here at me...ohhh! God! He's reaching for...what? That's a fanny pack...not a pistol stuffed in his waist band? Oh!! I thought this...

Rude Boys

*"Who the punk now boy...who the punk...who the
punk..."*

Marquise said it wasn't until the boy gave him the
finger that he went off. I guess the young'un thought
that his Hummer was something; he didn't know that
this truck had an 8 with dual carbs, we got up on him
in a flash then cut him off...just like he'd done us. The
back of that boy's Hummer had all these stickers on
it...like the punk rockers have on their hand-painted
rides. He had shit on there like, "Official Malcolm X
Fan Club, Black Panther Party Member" (complete
with that picture of Huey sitting in that rattan chair)
and some other stuff that offended both of us. None of
'em could know the first thing about any of the images
that they're sportin' and extolling. "Who the punk now
boy...who da punk...who the punk..." thumping out of
the oversized bass speakers. He jumped out of that truck
so fast that there wasn't time for me to do anything but

watch. The darkened windows didn't seem to influence him one bit as he grabbed the door handle and pulled the young driver out of the seat to the ground. By the time his posse drew down on him, he had blinked them both out.

"Who the punk now boy…who the punk…who the punk…" was the first sound he heard when he realized he wasn't on the side of 295 anymore.

"Who the punk now boy…who the punk…who the punk…" words not from "The Death Squad 1", but words out of the mouth of the biggest of the rednecks that surrounded him. "You must be one o'dem northerners. A trouble maker, our niggras down here don't like ya'll coming down here agittatin', this big one said with a deep drawl. "Who the hell are you", the youngun' said. With that, the shotgun buttcrashed into his mouth, sending teeth splashing to the ground. "Jr… this young'un needs to learn who he should stick his finger out to. Now which finger was it that you wanted me to see", as he pulled out the skinning knife from the sjeath. "This 'en here", as he cut off the tip of the young'un's index finger, with the razor-sharp blade. "Or was it these?", as he sliced deeply in his other fingers. Tears sprung from his young eyes, though not a sound escaped his lips. How had he arrived here in this place, where were his boys…they were just in the ride…where is the ride? Who are these people, and where is that fool that tried to bum-rush me? Finger? I didn't give that cracker any finger. I gave that old Negro the finger, then he bumrushed the ride like he wanted something, that's when the fellas drew down on him, we just, I mean, I just…

…A heel to his stomach brought him back to the matters at hand. "Who da punk now boy…who the punk…who the punk…" "Oh I think you wanted to tell me somethin'…what that finger means?" At that he sliced the blade through the waistband of the baggy pants until his boxer shorts were exposed. "Whose pants you got on boy? Yo Daddy's?"

At this moment, a truck passed by, an old truck, but it didn't seem old, wait, all of these cars and trucks are old, but recent. Am I in the 30's he thought? Look at their clothes. The cold steel blade of the knife caressed his testicles as a shot rang out. Shards of the pearl handle of the knife showered the young'un's face. "Next time ain't no warning shot. "Let him go…now," the man said as he stepped out of the car into full view, pistol in hand. It was the same crazy Negro who shouldered him off the road. How could this be. He was even dressed as they did back in the day. "Percy", the big redneck who cut the youngun said, "you ain't got nothin' to do wid this." "My name is Mr. Williams to you, boy and we look out after our own. Consider you and your drunk Daddy officially evicted from my property, as of now. That I do have something to do wid". Mr. Williams wrapped a handkerchief around the finger and applied pressure to stop the bleeding. "C'mon youngun, he said, I need to show you something". As they drove along in the truck for what seemed a long time the youngun said, "What you got to show me" The elder said, "all that". "All what", the youngun said. The elder blinked and said, "all that has passed before us, all that." In a blur, the youngun saw generations of people struggle to get to where we are now, the sacrifices, the concessions, the hope of the future, when the present seemed so hellish.

"We stand on the shoulders of giants. That's what makes us tall and proud. Not what you got and what you don't. You can't but culture, can't fake manners and good upbringing. You will always get what you always got, if you always do what you always did". And with that he blinked his eyes again and they were back on 295. Youngun's boys stood in awe and wonder with their guns at their sides not believing what they collectively had experienced. The youngun looked at his hand and didn't see blood, wounds or any marks. The Elder backed away from them to his truck returning their stares, blinked and drove away.

Apt. 803

Now, let me see if I got this right...this is only what I was told.

When they got there, after the maze of the parking lot and then the hallways, the woman said, "Well, I guess you all could go up to Apt. 803, I guess...how many of ya'll is there again?" As they exited the elevator, "*Mama cooked a chicken thought it was a duck, put it on the table with it's legs sticking up!*" was coming out of the stereo system at the door of Apt. 803. Female laughter, the just –a-little-overboard kind, the kind that goes with, laughing-at-anything-he-says-to-be-thought-of-as-cute, kind, was heard over the music. Sure enough, there's two women and one man sitting at the kitchen table, drinking. Single-parent apartment. The living room had been turned into a bedroom with a giant bed and TV/stereo system. The hard core entertaining type. The bed and the system. The sister's apartment, it appeared to be, said, "Come on in and well, Pur-cell...you gonna get outta here so these ladies can get dressed, so they can change into there…there… outfits…or whatever?" Purcell made no move at all, upon seeing these African Queens unexpectedly; he wasn't going no-where. In fact, wild animals couldn't make him. Per-cell you gonna have to excuse yo'self now! The bedroom they were directed to, to change, belonged to her son, typical young boy's room. These eight women couldn't have changed in the only restroom that was on the party room floor, that's why this Apt. 803, was suggested. Her friend wouldn't mind, the lady downstairs said. Good idea, tight, but they now had a bathroom and a bedroom to change in. In this space… this space that became the focal point of energy, as yet harnessed, to be released through the metamorphosis of music and dance, to those suspecting and un-.

When they first arrived, the Master Drummer was saying something to them in the hallway, something as to what was going on…something to the effect that the police had already visited while they were warming up! Police! Warming up…whoa! He said they were playing soft…and the man was called. There might be cause for concern, 'cause the party room is situated just down the hall from the security station. You can see them from the room, let alone they *can* hear the music. So, when

58

the complaints started coming down from the tenants of this lush Condo, they had to act accordingly. This is when the sponsors of the gig decided to read the small print in the contract they signed re: the room's usage... **No musical instruments/no live music.** "Get ready 'cause here I come...get ready 'cause here I come".

As they exited from Apt. 803, dressed in their grand Boubas, the color and texture of the fabric, rich beyond measure, two white guys in the hall stepped back in awe and wonder and said what Purcell couldn't..."Wow! You guys look great!" One of the women asked while they were waiting for the elevator, "Did anyone get a good look at the space beforehand? No one did? No one got a look?" They should have known then that they were to dance in a band box. Maybe that was giving it too much space. Tight. Tight like oops and 'scuse me. The "oops", as in oops...sorry, I'm all on top of you... again, and 'scuse me...for 'scuse me...was that your face my elbow hit? But the dancin' was hot! I heard tell temperatures were rising...and all them sisters said later that they were trying not to put to much... you know...into it...you know comin' from the root chakra-kind of into it...*but it was hot!* It was hot and movin' and the music was *good*...the kind that makes you say "fuck it…call the police", 'cause…"party ovah here, ya'll". The audience remembered these beats and rhythms, this ancient music. Thousands of years old, they remembered the dance and the words, but couldn't put it with where they first learned it. They said things like, "they'd never seen anything like this before…but it was familiar". Or, "it made my skin get goose-pimply, like just before you get the spirit". These were words coming from the elders, the ones that experienced first-hand the Jim Crow and segregation of this country. They were the ones that were on the front line of disavowing any and all that was African or reminders of that culture. They were raised with "act your age not your color", "coffee will make you black" and the adage, "if you're white, you're alright, if you're brown stick around, but if you're black get back." These elders were whooping and hollering with the dancers and the drummers. A part of the proceedings, not apart: distant and aloof. This music, these dancers, spoke of years bridged, languages remembered and rituals forgotten and now rekindled. Healing, repairing, mending, renewing, fortifying, strengthening. It's not how long something or someone is lost, it is the joyous expression of discovery that the heart knows and feels.

Once forbidden and often hidden, this sound of our ancestors miraculously is still being taught with the language of the dance and the sound of the words that marry the rhythm to the beat.

As the police stayed by the door to make sure that the last sound had been played, the members of the group that invited them for this Kwanza celebration were alive with the spirit of the ancestors. They vowed to bring them back to a place and a space where they could enjoy them and experience them to all's satisfaction. They would spread the word to their churches, community groups, social clubs and the like. This *is* the music, dance and words that were missing from this or that function, they all said. This is how it was done. This is how it was done for our forbearers; this is how it will be done for our future. From time before, to time everlasting.

Somebodysayyeah!

They Could Make it Rain

The ball landed at her feet, when her eyes looked up, Julie? Raych? They knew each other's names; it was the first word on each other's mind. They'd never met and didn't know where they'd known each other from, not initially. When he came bounding up to get the ball, he looked into Julie's eyes and went straight into her arms. They kissed like lost lovers, found. Which they were, but not in anyway they knew. Raychel wasn't fazed by this, he'd been a co-worker for years and she assumed that she knew her thru him. When they broke their embrace, their eyes still twinkling, "who are you" calmly Julie asked, in the most encompassing way. Right now I don't know, he said. And he certainly didn't. All three looked at each other in such a different light, then, realized something extraordinary had just happened. There had been no sounds in the air, and each thought they held was clear and purposeful, if that was the direction of the thought.

What is this…they all said…mentally…that took them by such surprise that they all started laughing at once because of this occurrence. Not a civil, dainty polite laugh, but a something funny, guffaw, side- splitter, tear-jerker. When they caught their breath between the oohs and ahhs, and "don't say no mores" they all hugged and introduced themselves. He and Julie never let go of each other's hand for the rest of the day. Raych seemed to be right there with them as if hanging in balance between them, even though it was impossible to actually get between them. They never split up after that as far as I know. They were something, they could make it rain.

When ever asked how they met, Julie and Raych always said, we knew each other's name before we knew each other. He and Julie were always together. You couldn't play a game where those two were teamed up…'cause you'd lose and badly. Cards, darts, once in a charades game from a clue he'd given, Julie got the answer in less than 5 seconds. "Reach for the falling stars but never for a falling knife" You know the one who gives the clues isn't the one that writes them… but he gives the best clues, she whined…as everyone groaned and then quit.

The majority of their work though was healing. One by one the "three" quit their day jobs to focus on what they were guided to do…heal, physical wounds, spiritual matters, and psychic phenomenon. They brought people out of comas, righted imbalances and grounded those in need. They could open up some chakras and glean out that stuff that gets backed up inside us sometimes…you know that kind of stuff… that old suit in your mind that used to fit so good back when that kind of thinking was in style…that you're still hanging on to. They reminded us to let it go, get a new suit, in today's style that fits…to feel good about ourselves. They could make it rain.

You know those little whirly things that come from trees? They helicopter down? We were sitting in the yard and one of them gets the thing to hover above the ground, never touching down. The others thought that was amusing and with their combined energies they played with those things all afternoon. They got them to whirl the other direction, hang suspended in midair, all kinds of things. This focused energy and playful experimenting led them to some discoveries that were spellbinding. Their combined energies began to create phenomenon that went off the belief scale. To understate it…you had to be there. Small cloud formations hovered over their garden, 4 or 5 feet off the ground…miniature clouds, a scaled down model of what was in the sky. They could get them to rain on demand, or dissipate or billow…it was something to see. As this discipline grew they became more centered and earthy. Their powers soared; remember the flood in St. Louis a few years ago? Mother Earth showing her might…yea…with the aid of some of her children. If they love her, it is her children's responsibility to help her in her changes, they spoke. Floods in the Dakotas, tornadoes in Miami, earthquakes in North Carolina. It's nothing to create a funnel they say, mix enough of the energy that's readily available and presto you have what is already out there, made manifest. I asked them why trailer parks got the brunt of so much destruction… they laughed till they cried at some sort of inside joke that I was never made privy to.

When they started chasing these huge twisters through the Midwest, I began to think they had reached the brink of sanity and had entered the danger zone. I was aware that they spoke of these twisters in terms that I had never associated with something of that sort. Reverence might be the closest in the English language that I could use to describe it. They didn't revere them as much as they "cowboyed" them…if I can use that term. They rode with them as if they were riding them, lassoing them to some cordoned off area, then unleashing the fury of the wind, to reap it's vengeance with full force and abandon. The wake of destruction fueled them to heights unimaginable, as energy gains momentum it has the potential...

The often said oneness: is essence, creativity, purity, love and unlimited unbounded energy. That matter is neither created nor destroyed. They could make it rain.

Bird Talk

He was one of them dudes that was always working on something. The thing was he'd be working on stuff that didn't go together. He'd have things hooked up to his computer that wasn't meant to be hooked up like that. He had water that changed colors in those glass things that you used to see in the pharmacy window. He could always tell you when the moon was gonna rise, what time the tides come in, off the top of his head. What he could do that truly amazed me was he could fall asleep within, say 15 sec….no kidding. No, he didn't have narcolepsy: he could tune out that fast to another dimension, at will.

Back to his experiments, he had a flower that was hooked up to a silent whistle that woke his dog, to take the medicine that was left in his bowl. He said he figured that the flower emitted enough energy that could be harnessed. 'Sides, he said, I've never seen it asleep, it watches everything, and that dog is pretty smart - too. He made the wire-like connections that tethered one to another – also. Things he said conduct, that you'd never imagine. Corn...is widely misunderstood...it's a signaling device that has intergalactic ramifications. See...I'm starting to sound like him. Well, it's one of those "things" he was working on that finally worked. He even had a name for it...his "voss-romulator". In his conversations he'd use that name as a noun, then a verb, describing the actions someone did or didn't do. "They need their vos-romulator adjusted or repaired depending on the action witnessed.

He wrote in a binary fashion which enabled him to communicate with the chirping birds. He claimed he wasn't yet totally conversant with them, but he did understand the crux of their information passed on. This led him to write in a binary fashion. He could then read it and transcribe their messages literally. Made me take notice about how chirping takes on another meaning when you focus on the changes in warble, pitch, tempo and meter. Something is definitely being communicated. Back to these experiments...this side by side dimension he'd speak of allowed one to become "cloaked" Just like the device the "Klingon" starships had in Star Trek. Think of how cool that could be in flying past the cops, with his radar gun pointed at you, and then you disappear along with all the data – that you were ever here. No blip on the radar, no read – out, no nothing, not even back draft. How cool is that?

As his experiments with that concept got better and better, somehow it leaked out that he was doing these kinds of things. If you think our government is slow to respond, just start doing that kind of stuff and see how fast you'll get a reaction. You'll have black Suburbans with dark tinted windows at your doorstep in a blink of an eye. The first visitors were nosey neighbors, or so he thought. When he started having problems with his gas and electric service, more and more technicians would be needed to fix whatever problem that dragged on and on. He began to be concerned. This cloaking device also allowed him to reside in a parallel dimension where he could gather information unseen or unheard. Think about how valuable that little device could be in the right or wrong hands. He understood that, and realized that he couldn't remain in his present position, unaware. He was able to use them as they wanted to use him. Walking into NSA or Langley was no problem, it's that he didn't want their information or need it to further his work. Being informed of their intentions helped put him at an advantage. When or where they were gonna move helped him stay one step ahead of them.

The constricts and constraints of gravity forced him to embellish his experiments until he understood just what its use was. That was when things started to get out of hand, or in control, whichever way you want to view it. Just about every space that was available had something written on it. His binary script allowed him to have a continuous written conversation wherever he was, uninterrupted he claimed. It's like a good conversation that one can just jump in anywhere and be on the same page. If you think perpetual motion is unattainable or want to see the fallacy of Newton's third law, he could show you and explain what you just witnessed in a way that made sense. Does that make sense? It didn't to me until I saw with my own eyes what I just described. There's an old adage about, "what one can conceive, one can achieve". He proved that to the nth.

Shooter

The only thing she noticed as she walked into the room was his distant eyes. When they finally looked at her, they penetrated her thoroughly, she felt naked, wanted to cover herself up and he never took his eyes off her face. As she looked away, he went away, away from any connection that seconds ago had been established. After a few minutes of this silence and distance she asked if he had any plans for his future. "You don't want to know that", he responded. "You wouldn't know anything about that" he said coldly. "Try me, I'm a little smarter than I appear", she said. "A sniper", is all he said. You mean in the military, working for our government, she said a little too chipper even for her. Naw, he slowly replied, a private contractor, having history in my hands. See, I told you, you wouldn't know nothin' 'bout this. The look on her face betrayed her composure. A killer for hire, that's your inspiration? Yep, he breathed in a short breath, and this time he went away, far away. Austin, Texas, the book tower and scattering screaming people underneath. The shots ring out and the adrenalin starts to ooze, as the blood starts to flow, as the cordite lingers in the air from the hot spent rounds. It's on…hunting season. The fire alarm rings and the regularity of the drill marches everyone outside…as the shots ring out and the pandemonium spreads, adrenalin oozes and again the blood flows… it's the elixir. The experience of: the "all that I am/am not". Then the grin on his face freezes her in her tracks as she is about to leave the room. "Going so soon? I'll be out in a few minutes; you know they can't hold me any longer…I'll even walk you to your car, this neighborhood isn't what it used to be…can't be too careful." "No, it's not", she thought, "but am I safer with him"? As part of her repaying her student loan, she has to do mandated hours of pro bono work with juveniles at risk, first offenders or those on the brink of adjudication for minor offenses. It is the hardening lessons that all public defenders have to experience. The visions of saving the youth and turning lives around come to a complete halt with the most liberal hearted, after a few years of this type of service.

Uncommon Commonality

It all started with the sound of a motorcycle, revving loudly. Just as she began to think that the bike was getting awfully close, a hard shove in the back sent her reeling. The baby came flying out of her arms, up in the air. In one motion, the little Asian woman that shoved her, grabbed the baby and in a pirouette handed the baby back to the woman pushed. The woman pushed grabs the little Asian woman, encircling her arms around her and pulls her forward. The out of control bike passed inches from where they were just standing. They both ended up in the potato bin of the corner Green Grocer.

The baby was nestled safely between them, oblivious to the undertakings. Xiu Li, never one to be mistaken for anyone's hero had just saved this woman and baby's life. Consuelo, without thinking, had just saved this woman's life. It happened in a blur of time, yet, each of them acted so in the moment that time stood still. As they got to their feet, this chance meeting cemented them to each other. In their native tongues, they both began to speak excitedly about what had taken place.

Each thanked the other and both began their description of this happenstance. This chat wasn't the usual shy and unassuming banter. They went on and on for over an hour. Neither one could understand the actual words the other was saying, but this didn't hinder the dialog they both developed. They laughed at each other's jokes, looked deeply into each other's eyes and sparks flew. Friends bonded right there on this New York City, street corner. They both told of being in this new city just two weeks and being au pair's for their sisters. The incredible thing is that the baby never once cried out and after the first minutes of their conversation, language never got in their communicative way.

They called each other on the phone and laughed at how odd their conversations would start, until they'd find their rhythm and click...then they'd be chatting like school girls again...not knowing the words mind you, but deeply understanding the thought and meaning. They began ESOL classes together and this only accelerated their communication. Each day they had another group of language thoughts they could use to access each other. How closely tied these two cultures were indeed. Both of these young women agreed that change was necessary in their male dominated societies.

The mix of Chinese, Spanish and English created a unique language that these two developed. Consuelo saw a poetry slam on cable and mentioned it to Xui Li, what developed was off the hook. Rumba meets tea ceremony; it was the sound of wind chimes to a conga beat. Bamboo flute to twelve string guitars, palm trees and rice cakes. Dim Sum, with cassava, and yellow rice. Nobody could figure them out; you couldn't talk about them in any language, at least not the three languages they now spoke. But you could guarantee that they would talk about you in theirs. Consuelo taught Xui Li how to bring it from the root and was in turn taught how to bring it from the third eye. Far East meets Caribbean.

The Session

You wanna feel that phone book upside your head again? I'm tired of this horseshit you're feeding me. I want you to tell me again and I want the whole story. You take your time and tell me all that went down, or I'm locking your ass up for obstruction…you got that? *Yeah I got it. What am I gonna say this time that I haven't already said?* I'm just getting used to the fact that it happened at all, how am I gonna get them to at least understand that it could possibly happen? *Yeah, yeah,* I said to the good cop of the good cop/bad cop duo that was interrogating me, *I'll tell you what happened, if you don't believe me, that's your problem.*

I had just joined the band a coupla months before and went out on tour with them to a few cities, when we got back to New York the bass player said he'd had enough and quit…cold…no warning…no notice. We had a general call for players we knew and while we were auditioning them, the drummer gets real sick and has to be rushed to the hospital. Now no bass and no drummer, well this chick who was there said she used to play drums and could fill in till we finished auditioning bass players. Nothing frilly just a steady beat was what we called for, this skinny kid jumps up and says that he'd like to play with her...like it was her band or something. Before I could call out the tune they were in it...like they'd played with us for years, all the changes all the little things we'd do to fill out the song, it was amazing. Next we'd just call out key changes and they were doing this modal thing that kept the beat and time while we filled in the rest. *You know anything about music? Sly and Robbie? Chambers and Philly Joe? Well they're legendary.* These two started playing like they'd known each other all their lives. It took us all by surprise that they'd just met. Drums and bass is the rhythm section, if that ain't happening nothin' is. They were happenin' in a big way. He'd start this lick and she could anticipate where they were going with it, you know how someone finishes the sentences of someone else? This is what they could do musically and as I told you...in other ways. This is how it all started...as I can remember. She wasn't there to audition as I found out later, a friend of hers played bass, but he didn't get a chance to be heard. When these two started to play it was evident that they were meant to play together.

You know how old couples finish the ends of each others sentences; well they started doing that from the beginning, 'til they just stopped talking out loud altogether. They would sit back to back like kids at a picnic, then go into the studio and create the most amazing sounds anyone had ever heard. She said that true knowledge was stored in stone and bone; this is how they were connected. They would do this chant-like thing, she'd begin then he'd join in. oh yeah, I forgot the spinning thing they 'd do, they'd spin around like whirling dervishes, something like 99 times, three sets of 33. Then they would stop and place their hands in front of themselves one hand on each others hand like in prayer. This created an illusion when you watched, kinda like they would go out of focus for awhile. I don't think they were lovers, but they were closer than any lovers I'd ever known. Looking into each others eyes they found things that we on the outside could only guess. After some time they stopped talking altogether, not to us but to each other. They'd be on the bus holding hands, or shoulder to shoulder and then crack up as if someone had told the funniest joke. It was communication on the highest level I'm sure. If you came between them you could feel the incredible energy, it flowed like a river, and you at once knew different languages, things you knew you never knew, but couldn't explain. The sounds that you felt first inside, then heard, would come out as if they were the finest tones one could experience. Put all of this together and one day they said to us in rehearsal, watch this...they started a chant added bass and drums, then they went out of focus and were gone, but the tone remained in the air, not the music, just the tone, from somewhere way off. Finally this was happening so regular that we took it for granted, then one day they didn't return. That, was what happened, I was in the sound booth and saw them with my own eyes, for what I guess now was the last time. They didn't run away or get kidnapped; they just blinked out of this dimension, that's the best way for me to explain it.

The phone book slammed into my head...again, this time with more deliberate force. After my ears stopped ringing and the tears left my eyes, I focused on the one who struck me and all he said was...book him...for obstruction.

Three Stories

The three of them didn't know it had happened already…they each said that they had gone to sleep the night before with the wish that something meaningful, something deep would happen in their lives…shit… even something freaky, alien abductions, time-dimensional traveling. They each got their wish.

Ted

It took Ted a few days before it hit him, and it hit him hard. He was in the mirror shaving and he got it with such clarity that his image in the mirror winked at him…and it didn't freak him out. He'd been dealing off and on in Eastern Buddhist philosophy and dogma. What intrigued him the most was the idea of getting rid of 'desire'. When that is obtained, nirvana is right there. He'd seen a Star trek episode where Kirk, Bones and Spock were caught in a force field and the harder you fought to get out of it, the more pressure you felt as a result. Well, cool-ass Spock figured that whole thing out in seconds, gave up all desire and waltzed right out.

In the meanwhile, Kirk and Bones are being crushed by the immense pressure being exerted by their will/ desire. They're getting flattened like a press…from everywhere, all because they wouldn't give up their desire to go toe to toe with this mirroring force field. Spock is walking in and out of the force field showing 'em how simple it's constructed, "Elementary" he's saying. Don't give it any energy he's telling 'em. When Ted saw that episode, he thought…"yeah, that' it… that it…don't give any of this any energy, and you can start to see what it is." He was changed immediately… phone rings…not the house, but his cell…it was 7:00 in the morning. "Let me say this to you, I'm not your plaything, I'm the best thing to happen to you, in your life. Whatchu gonna do? I told you I'm not tryin' to be on nobody's contraceptives…I'm tryin' to be in a family way. I mean family and I mean all the way. When ted's ears caught their breath, he had to remember to breathe. The no energy idea headed straight through the suicide window. You could hear it falling and crying…you didn't even ttrrryyyy. Ted gave up big energy, Yolanda. Whas wrong widdchu? Why you trippin' so much, so early? At that, he thought of hanging up and she replied coolly…You hang up on me and you hang up on us.

Then, for the next 10 mins., he'd think it and she'd respond. He knows his lips weren't moving 'cause his hand was over his mouth. His skin had goose pimples, if he had any hair on the back of his neck, it would have been standing up. Tears streamed down his face, he'd pissed himself...he was terrified! Is this really happening? He slapped the shit out of himself...no he wasn't dreaming, that shit hurt. He thought, what's going on...what's going on? Yolanda replied. He was so overwhelmed he put both hands to his face...this power scared the shit of him, as the phone was dropping to the floor, Yolanda was saying, Look, I probably came at chu in a way that...I'll call you laterrrrrr...as the phone hit the floor. Ted called for his Momma (who'd recently passed) appeared right there...Hey Pookie...she said. He saw her over his right shoulder and fainted. Hit the floor like a sack of dropped potatoes.

Ayyana

As the front door closed, Ayyana was tryin' to remember to breathe. Was she holding a check for

$47,372, in her hand? And did those people really tell her they didn't expect her to play any more numbers or scratch-offs for the next 18 months? Were they/was that a threat? It sure felt like it. Lottery officials, they left hats and pens and all that. This chat was after the big cardboard check photo-op. The big handsome guy had my arm gripped up like I was a booster...caught. It wasn't my fault I've been lucky with numbers and scratch-offs. First, the scratch-offs would win me money for another scratch-off. Then, I'd just see 'em, could feel the winners that became routine. Then the numbers came through my Aunt Bessie, in my dreams. She was my favorite Auntie. Got killed with my Uncle in a car accident, a drunk driver hit them head-on. They say they never knew what hit 'em. We never would say good-bye, she'd say "every good-bye ain't gone", but she'd visit me in my dreams so often I could talk to her as if she was right here. She even taught me (in my dreams) how to run fast and how to quit falling. Now that was something. I started watching the numbers and they'd come out, sometimes in DC, sometimes in Md. Or Va., but they'd come out...boxed, straight, in Pick 4's...but they'd be right. It was no science, just Aunt Bessie. So the little money I'd scrape together, I'd hit every week on something. It got so, last summer I gave notice and walked out of that corporate shit of a job. I haven't looked back and here in my hands is the most money I've ever had at one time in my life.

Rasheed

Rasheed knows that he should be dead, twice…the same night. He stood up, turned to put the flat tire in the trunk and the tractor trailer came by his face no more than an inch. The force of the speeding semi knocked him onto the hood. As he was trying to remember to breathe…his thoughts were wild with…"I could've just died." How the tire got flat was something in itself. As he came through the intersection a speeding car ran through the light from his right and his instincts made him slam on his brakes and sent the car into a 180 degree spin. The force of that peeled the tire right off the rim. He sat in the car for a few minutes getting himself together, remembering to breathe. As he stepped out of the car no one was on the street, in either direction. He bent down and examined the wheel, opened the trunk and pulled out the spare. While he was changing the tire, he returned mentally to the gathering he'd just left. His cousins, Ted and Ayyana had experienced the same moment. They were toasting their glasses in their Uncle's back yard and as they clicked them together, the biggest meteor they'd ever seen, streaked through the sky. They looked at each other but didn't say a word. In their nervous laughter they again raised their glasses to herald that event and three separate but smaller meteors shot by in an after mass. "Wow" was all they could say. This toast was the culminating event to the conversation they had been having as they sat by the pool. Each said that they wanted to experience something that, without a doubt, would prove to them that there was indeed some "other-worldly" presence in their lives. These first cousins were sitting and chatting about the life of their recently deceased, Aunt Bessie, and the events that brought them to this location, both physically and spiritually. The meteors were the signs that they all needed to signal that the evening was over and that something was happening, remember to breathe and they would promise to keep in touch in the days to come. As he stood up to put the tire into the trunk the force of the semi knocked him on the hood. A mere step in into the street would have killed him instantly. He could still feel the wake of air from that speeding mass of machinery. Wow.

The Viewer/The view

As he opened his eyes on the gurney he could see the lifeless form lying next to him. He wasn't supposed to be a twin let alone an identical one. This was their way of letting him out...so to speak...of the loop. He told me he first got a clue from some "B" movie he'd seen about an alien takeover. If you had a pair of some special sunglasses you could see the perpetration of the mind wash going down. Without them you were like so many sheep. Anyway, they figured it was best to grant him this request than run the risk of him becoming an underground teacher. Back in the early days they'd underestimated the effect a group of rebel teachers and counter- cults could have on their "*total indoctrination program*". The "**T.I.P.**" of the iceberg as the older ones put it. They don't take anything for granted these days. Remember how back in airline travel days they didn't stand for any comments to be made re: hijackings? Well take that to the nth level now, regarding just about anything.

When he originally made his request, the soldier on duty didn't have the clearance to handle that kind of thing. That is why so long a period of time went by before he could be *"processed"*. There is still some darkness about who and where he was for those first hours. A Level One alert immediately went into effect when it was made clear who and what said what to whom. Top level officials were awakened of out their slumbers, and rightly so. To miss out on the rare opportunity to glimpse one of the originals was more than most could bear.

The power and magnetism of this individual was something to behold, though none were brave enough to experience it outside of the chamber. They didn't want to run the risk of being contaminated by his thoughts and psychic abilities. This request of his was a small consolation for what could have been catastrophic on their part. The fact that he had survived and flourished these many years is a testament to the power that was always rumored these kind of people had. It was said it had been many days before they saw him take any nourishment. He refused to indulge any of the sustenance they'd offered. Instead he would chant and bring his metabolic rate down to where now it was legal to pronounce him dead. Again it was so rare to happen upon one of these that the processing centers were working out an effective counter-to the ever present rumors of their exploits. Though these rumored exploits were becoming less and less. I should say at this point, in all fairness, that they were being *reported* less and less. Everyday occurrences were witnessed and experienced by those who were in-tune, not indoctrinated, living in the outskirts or those who simply were unplugged, and living on their own power. They wished they knew where and why he decided to surface. The pieces to this complex puzzle didn't seem to fit. The request that he made to them wasn't as unusual as it appears. They now will never know why. As it was once said...the deed is done.

It wasn't until the complete cloning was finished that they realized that all the information that was in him could not be transferred into their computer/brain banks. They also do not know if this information was completely transferred to him. This is the area of great concern. It has become a national security risk. That is the reason for all of the monitoring. The most reliable and exact measure would require human intervention and one-on-one contact. At this level, that is not an option. Cerebral sleuthing is what this could be called, except it's partly on the telepathic and psychic side. That would require that a person to examine him would have to open up themselves in order to get close enough, to ascertain the depth of knowledge and transferred information. None of the officials on duty were interested in this type of trade. It would be a small price indeed if this was the only fall-out from this encounter. When the program was first instituted, there was an immediate rash of literature on subliminal persuasion, and mind control. The media access was the initial key in distancing the thinking public from the thought barons. The control of the media allowed them to ridicule all that were on the path to discovery of their "total indoctrination program", thus eliminating all comers. The rebel teachers and underground cults allowed the only dissension, thus their elimination was of the first order. Through the use of the media: nutrition, health practices and basic beliefs were programmed into the populace. This allowed the careful tuning of certain frequencies to affect the behavior and reactions of individuals. When certain pulses and impulses were triggered there was a conditioned response that went into play. After awhile the norm was for the masses to react in this way. This is how many of the others were discovered, by their non-reaction to the impulses. Though everyone resembled each other, it was by subtle responses that the "shining" ones were revealed. This may be one reason why there has been an increase in the use of sunglasses, even at night. At one time it was considered a sign of sincerity to look into the person's eyes you were talking to, now it is a sign of another time, gone by. He offered no resistance when first interviewed, but that is the trademark of those with the "gift", and before you realize it you're over on the other side. No one wanted to be the one to be turned... not after all of this time, not now that they had become used to and conditioned to all of this. It wasn't worth it to experiment now. If he retained it all, so be it that *was* their problem.

He looked around as he regained his composure and thought of the process that he'd just completed. He wasn't sure that what he'd undertaken would kill him. It hadn't, but what had it done. The mental checklist that took microseconds, reminded him of what there was yet to do. The body on the matching gurney looked just like him, but then again, nothing like him at all. The human form was the only reminder of the work that was at hand. Slowly, he began to feel himself regenerating and renewing. The cacophony of sounds from the other side of the partition began to stimulate his hearing senses. It was time. Rising and answering their questions at once...all at once, quieted them to a dull hush. How had he done that? There were more than fourteen languages being spoken at the same time. As if on queue, they realized that they'd been had and before they could say or do anything, he rose from the gurney, faced them, waved and winked good-bye, and restructured his atomic alignment and was gone.

Made in the USA
Charleston, SC
29 March 2010